a devotional book for

strength in our

uncertain times

Lee Ann Layson

Dear Reader,

Over the years I have discovered that reading Christian devotional books, at least those that are written in a personal style with which I can connect, help me in my meditative time spent with God. However, I understand that devotional books cannot substitute for the Bible, but are a good support and supplement in helping us all to relate to God's word. I hope these devotionals and prayers bring you comfort. Not surprisingly, these writings still minister to me whenever I go back and read them. The Holy Spirit is a Comforter and a Guide, and without His inspiration, the following work would have never come about in the first place. Just as a note of special interest, there is also a prayer of salvation at the end of the book for those who would like to claim a personal relationship with Jesus Christ. May God bless you and keep you!

Lee Ann Layson

Souls in danger look above

Jesus completely saves.

He will lift you by His love

Out of the angry waves.

He's the Master of the sea

Billows His will obey

He your Savior wants to be

Be saved today.

Love lifted me!

Love lifted me!

When nothing else could help

Love lifted me!

"Love Lifted Me" lyrics by James Rowe

1. "Love Lifted Me"

Sometimes no matter how hard we try at being "good" Christians, we find ourselves spiraling downward into dark murky waters. Unless some sort of intervention follows or somehow we are able to supernaturally swim rapidly upwards, all sorts of negative feelings flood us and we wonder if we will ever see the light of day again. That's where The Light comes in. Jesus says in John 14:18-27: "I will not leave you as orphans…Peace I leave with you; My peace I give to you; I do not give to you as the world gives. Do not let your hearts be troubled and do not be afraid."

Although Jesus died over two thousand years ago, He was resurrected from the cross. He did not stay in His tomb. God's Word is ever living, ever breathing. Jesus still lives and He loves all of us. No matter how abandoned we feel, even right now, this moment, we are *not* alone.

My life, like most people's, has had its moments of trepidation, sadness and loneliness. We probably all have been there way too often. But what has saved me time and time again is God's love and comfort. In fact, we can each find comfort by the love God provides through others, even people we might not normally think of as ones providing God's heavenly services or being true servants of God.

For instance, I once was in a terrible accident. My right leg was severed half-way through. Glass imbedded my face, arms and legs. I was in shock. After I had been left on the emergency room table alone and terrified, my surgeon arrived, Dr. Nestor Montero. His eyes were soft pools of kindness. At last! My heart rejoiced. Someone who cares! As he tended my needs and asked pertinent questions, he looked intently into my eyes. "You should have died, you know," he stated emphatically. "God must have a special purpose for saving you. Do not forget."

A special purpose? I wondered, thrilled that perhaps angels sent by God had been instrumental in saving me at the last moment. What was my special purpose? Well, as time went by and times seemed to move from peril to peril, I began to question the wisdom of my doctor. Had he just been sharing platitudes? Was I saved only to continue my pathway of suffering?

No, I was saved to be His servant. Maybe you have been as well? Everybody suffers. It is what we do with our pain that makes all the difference. Will we let it define us or refine us? No matter what our questions might be about concerning the "Why?" of our trials and what feels like fierce, never-letting-up opposition, love is the answer, our solution to our problems. His undying love for us always is….and we must never forget that, especially when times turn their darkest. It is then we need Him the most.

Prayer:

Dear Heavenly Father,

We know You have told us that we are never alone, but sometimes we feel alone anyway. You have told us that You are the light in our darkness, but still we are often unable to grapple our way to Your love and Your hope. We know our fears bind us, and when we focus on our problems instead of You, we are magnifying our problems instead of magnifying You.

Please help us to realize that no matter how bad things get, You are indeed with us. You are The Solution if we will but stop and have the faith to accept it and come to You with our hearts' pains and our aching need for solace.

Amen

2. "My Logic is Illogical"

I don't know about you, but sometimes I just do some really stupid things. The negative outcome is obvious even before I make my poor decision, but for whatever reason, I do not perceive it or I will not accept its reality and I blunder right on into my decision's un-escapable conclusion.

For example, I struggle with my weight. I know I have a tendency to binge on snacks and to eat large portions at meal times if I have waited too long to eat or if I am tired, frustrated or stressed.

There are certain foods that I realize are too great a temptation for me to have around, and yet, I rationalize the buying of the treats for "the children" to enjoy, for it isn't their fault, I argue, that I have a strained relationship with food.

Sadly, this decision to be "fair" bites me back as I devour the snacks I promised myself I was purchasing or cooking for my children and husband. Sure…like I didn't know *that* was going to happen….

Why, then, am I surprised and hurt when I step on the scales and my weight has skyrocketed?

Duh.

Unfortunately, many people in our society today perform similar self-defeating rituals. But for them, the temptation may be sex, gambling, shopping, drinking, drugs… I could list many more possible problem areas, and I bet you could add some more to this list as well.

The warning signs that our choices are about to lead us into a miserable pit of our own creation are normally fully evident, but we plunder on, oblivious to where our choices are leading us: certain disaster. We become defensive when people ask us why we would make such obviously self-destructive decisions. We are dumbfounded as well at ourselves and at our inability to make sense of our own actions. Sure, hindsight is 20-20, but how can we at times be so blind, or worse, refuse to acknowledge what we do see? God warns in Psalm 32:8-9:

I will instruct you and teach you

in the way you should go:

I will counsel you and watch over

you.

Do not be like the horse or the mule,

which have no understanding

but must be controlled by bit and

bridle….

Guidance is indeed there for the taking and for the applying in Scripture if we are so inclined to take advantage of its holy wisdom and direction. Yet, how many times have I been that senseless mule who stubbornly plods toward disaster? Maybe you have been a little mulishness before in your ways? It happens. But it does not have to.

Thank goodness that there is hope when we fail, hope when we foolishly attempt to mold our own lives instead of allowing the Potter to shape us. The writer of Psalm 30 cries, "O Lord my God, I called to you for help and you healed me…You spared me from going down into the pit" (2-3). What a relief that God does have new mercies for us every morning if we will but go to Him for the asking of His grace.

Prayer:

Dear Heavenly Father,

We know we have been more stubborn in our behavior more times than we would like to admit to anyone, especially, You. Yet, as much as we would love to defend our actions, there is no argument in our defense, no way of deceiving You that we were justified in our behavior. We have refused to do what was right and we have ignored Your gentle guidance's tugging at the reins of our hearts. Still, You have not treated us as we have deserved. Thank You for Your love and Your absolute forgiveness. Please help us to remember that if we love You like we say we do, we will obey You when You ask us to do something. Period. No discussion. No half-hearted attempts at obedience.

Amen

3. "Where Are The Snacks?"

Before we moved to where we live now, we were members of a local town Presbyterian church and it was its theology that if a parent believed a child understood and embraced the undertaking of Communion, and if he or she had been baptized, the child could participate in this sacrament. I really do not remember now exactly what age my daughter Rachel was at this time. She was probably around nine, old enough, I thought, to understand the basic concepts. So, after much spiritual preparation, she participated in her first communion experience.

Things went well, and Rachel soberly accepted the elements in quite the mature fashion. On the way home from church we reflected once more on the significance of Communion, and she seemed to have all the "right" answers for my questions that reassured me that she did indeed understand, at least at a foundational level, what the service symbolized…that is until the following Sunday.

Yes, it was then when I realized I had been totally clueless to my daughter's understanding of what Communion was all about (It was not to be the last time I was clueless as a parent). We had just adjusted ourselves into the pew and marked our hymns as cited in the bulletin. As I looked up, I noticed Rachel's concerned expression of alarm. She eyed the empty table in front of the preacher's podium that had borne the elements the previous Sunday and whispered urgently, "Mom! Where are the snacks?"

As the years passed, I gleaned similar stories from friends and acquaintances. Their children or grandchildren had also asked about the disappearance of the "snacks" as well the Sunday after their own first communions or at least soon thereafter. Why there had been an obvious communication breakdown with all of our children, I could only surmise.

Sometimes we, too, when it comes to the Bible, just don't get the basic concepts even though we think we have it all figured out or we suppose we understand enough of its general premises to get the basic themes and morals we believe it implies. Praying to God on a regular basis is erratic at best, but we do remember to go to God when we have an urgent matter that we need resolved. Why is it that we hate to be used or taken for granted, but we so *easily* take God for granted? It makes no sense.

Indeed, Proverbs 3:5-6 advises, "Trust in the Lord with all your heart and lean not on your own understanding; in all your ways acknowledge Him, and He will make your paths straight." How many times have I wandered off His path or arrogantly tried to make my own way without asking God first if it is *His* way? Prayer is preventive and proscriptive. So why do I so often forget?

Prayer-amnesia. I wonder how many people forget to pray for guidance? Sometimes we all decide our own pathways and then ask God to bless our plans or at least give us guidance down the paths we have chosen, not even bothering to ask God if the paths we have elected are the best, the ones He has chosen for us.

Wow. Sometimes for logical people, we do not act so logically. Praying is indeed the practical thing to do every single time, every single situation, not the last solution on the list of our order of problem-solving ideas. Obviously, it makes a lot more sense to prevent a problem than to create one.

Now, if I could only remember this and apply these words of wisdom to my *own* life…Ah, now there's the rub of it all! Knowing what is right is one thing. Doing what is right is something different entirely. Thank You, God, for Your endless patience!

Prayer:

Dear Holy Father,

Why is it we have such a hard time remembering to pray? We have no excuses for our forgetfulness except for complacency. When things are going OK, we often forget to pray. When things are going from bad to worse, we have no problem remembering. We pray. Please forgive us for taking You and Your blessings for granted. Forgive us for the times we have not even acknowledged the loving ways You show us You love us. We regret that we often don't include You in decisions we make which we realize shows a lack of trust in You. Please help us to stay in Your will and to be obedient to the call You have placed on our lives to do Your service in whatever shape or form Your service turns out to be.

Amen

4. "What's Love Got to Do With It?"

Boy, isn't Love an overused word in today's culture, so overused at times that it has lost its original meaning? "I loved the movie I saw last night!" we often hear people (or ourselves, for that matter) exclaim. "I'd love to lose a little weight," someone else might later lament on further down the conversation as the theme of discussion turns in a different direction. "Yeah, but I sure do love ice cream," another in the group might confess. "I hear you," one might respond. "I hate giving something up that I love."

But what does *love* have to do with this? Absolutely nothing.

John states in 1 John 3:16: "This is how we know what love is: Jesus Christ laid down His life for us. And we ought to lay down our lives for our brothers." Later John adds, "This is how God showed His love among us: He sent His one and only Son into the world that we might live through Him. This is love: not that we loved God, but that He loved us…."

I guess that says it all, doesn't it?

When my heart swells with emotion as I gaze upon my beautiful children, Rachel, who has grown up so very quickly, (Where did the time go?) and is now off discovering her life's purpose, and my two darling boys, Daniel and Christopher, who are evolving into men right in front of my very eyes, I cannot fathom the grief and agony God must have felt knowing how His sinless, perfect child would suffer to save His "other" adopted children (us), children so often disobedient and so often openly rebellious. Yet, somehow as unrighteous as we are, He felt we were worth it.

What does love have to do with this? Absolutely everything.

Prayer:

Dear Heavenly Father,

Thank You for modeling what true love is. Sometimes we are so casual with the word love without even realizing it. We trivialize the word when we should revere its usage with respect. Thank you for Your unconditional love and that You were willing to give up Your very own son even though You knew we would not deserve it, no matter how many times we attempted being “good.” Help us to truly learn how to love others instead of focusing on meeting our own needs first. Please teach us how to love others as You love.

Amen

5. "Are We Plugged In?"

I was setting up my computer in our dining room, my favorite room in the house, my place to read, write and pray. But, even though I knew I had plugged my computer in correctly into the electrical outlet (it's not like that takes much mental acuity), the computer, whose battery was out of juice, would not come to life. What is wrong, I wondered? I know the power is there. Why is it not making the connection to my computer?

Then I remembered. For this particular outlet, if I did not turn on the light switch across the room which turned on the light in the china cabinet, the outlet was not viable. Ah Hah!

I turned on the switch. The china cabinet was illuminated; all the family treasures of china and nick-knacks were proudly on display.

The computer worked.

It was finally plugged into to its source of power.

It's funny how sometimes we don't even realize we are about to run out of juice ourselves until we do. Huh? What's wrong with me? We ask ourselves. Why don't I have any energy? Why do I feel so "blah," so apathetic?

Then, if things go well for us, we remember how we've been so "productive" lately, too busy to read our Scripture or devotionals, too busy to pray, too busy going 100 miles an hour non-stop… too busy being busy. Then we suddenly come to the point where not only have we stopped, we cannot fathom how to begin again. What has happened?

Maybe as Christians, we just forget Who is in charge, and Who supplies the Power. (It's not us.)

Are we plugged in, plugged into the Source, the Holy Spirit? And how do we get plugged into the Spirit, anyway? Jesus once told His disciples, "But you will receive power when the Holy Spirit comes on you" (Acts 1:8).

"Yeah, but that was concerning the disciples a long, long time ago," we might respond. "He wasn't talking about us today!"

Was too. That same power is available for us as well. All we have to do is ask, and God will give us all the power we can handle from a source that never has to be recharged or replaced. God is Good!

…So, are we plugged in? It's time for a self-check.

Prayer:

Dear Heavenly Father,

Sometimes we feel so weary and lackluster. Things get us down. We have too much packed into our schedules and we always feel like we could use a nap, but no naps are in sight. Thank You that You know what we need before we even ask for it. Thank You for reminding us that you will renew our strength like an eagle's if we will just stop for a moment to ask for Your help. Thank You that we are not alone to face the world. You will never run out of compassion for us or abandon us as orphans in the world. You will never stop loving us and believing in us. Thank You Father.

Amen

6. "Peace Through God's Strength"

Peace Through God's Strength. Strength Through God's Peace. It may sound like a riddle or a puzzle, but it is not. What *is* puzzling is that sometimes we just don't get it. God has everything we need. He will provide peace when we need it and He will not only give us strength but be our Strength when we can barely whisper a desperate plea for help. Psalm 29 gives us much needed comfort: "The Lord gives strength to His people; the Lord blesses His people with peace (11).

I don't know if you are familiar with Psalm 29. This particular psalm focuses on God's magnificent strength and His power. Actually, so many of the psalms include the theme of God's power and protection. We can certainly feel at peace knowing God is here with us at all times.

Psalm 32 also discusses the all encompassing love that God wishes to bestow on us: "Many are the woes of the wicked, but the Lord's unfailing love surrounds the man who trusts in Him" (10). The psalmist is not inferring that God's Children do not have adversity or hard times. What he is stating quite clearly is that unlike the evil-doers who do not acknowledge God, we do not have to worry or feel lost when hard times hit because God is with us and He makes His presence known to those who love Him and cry out for His comfort. His are strong arms, arms that promise peace through their strength.

I remember being picked up by Daddy when I was a child pretending to be asleep on the sofa. He would place me in my bed and Mama would softly kiss me goodnight. Talking about a little heaven on earth…the love I felt emanating from my parents was so reassuring and comforting. I was deeply loved. I knew it for a fact. There was no doubt about that. God loves us just like this but magnified to an astronomical degree.

We can be at peace no matter how scary or tough times get. God is in control even if we don't understand that point clearly during the chaos and the madness sometimes that takes our breath away with its suddenness. Even then we can endure whatever comes our way because God's love and power is the assurance that we will "walk *through* the shadow of death" (Psalm 23). That is a Promise worth remembering. God keeps His Word.

Prayer:

Dear Holy Father,

Sometimes life is unbearably tough. Things seem bleak and hopeless. At least that's the way things seem until we remember You. We have to trust You and have faith that no matter what, You allow things bad or good to happen for a reason. Thank You for guiding our lives and giving us the support we need when we forget our blessings and focus on our circumstances. We praise You, Lord.

Amen

7. "How Deep Are Your Roots?"

But blessed is the man who trusts in the Lord,

whose confidence is in Him.

He will be like a tree planted in the

water

That sends out its roots by the stream.

It does not fear when heat comes;

Its leaves are always green.

It has no worries in a year of

drought

And never fails to bear fruit.

(Jeremiah 17: 7-8)

This scripture came to my mind the other day when I was out in the pasture behind our house. I had transplanted a volunteer Yoshino cherry close enough to our vegetable garden so I could easily water it and keep a watchful eye on its progress, and I did, that is, until our family left on a Florida vacation.

I bet you can guess where this is going…the tree died while I was gone.

I actually was surprised because the tree had seemed quite established. We had asked family to please help us with the watering of the garden, but I had never even worried for a second about my cherry tree. It was flourishing when I left. It was already dead when I got back in a week.

We had had no rain in Georgia while we were gone and the heat index had catapulted up past the 100 degree mark. My poor little cherry--its roots were too shallow to make it--so it was all over for the little guy. End of story.

However, although my little tree never had a chance, the tree in Jeremiah has it all figured out. Tap into the source of life, and all those thirst worries are over. Eternal Life is there for the receiving. Christ is our living water, the source of our lives and the source of our hope. In addition, we also have to trust Christ if we expect Him to reveal the fruits of the Holy Spirit to us.

Trust. It is that simple. Scripture says we should have no worries and lean not on our own understanding. Yet, in all honesty, I know I have often been disobedient due to my insistence on worrying about the "What Ifs" without asking God first what He thinks about my concerns. I have a strong feeling God doesn't stay up at night stressing out about uncertainties. Maybe I shouldn't either.

A tree tapped into a stream does not have to worry about having life; its source is its confidence. Christ is our Confidence, our source of stability if we will just allow Him to be that for us. We must believe that God *will* do what He says He *will* do. Truly, that is called faith. Please, Lord, help us to be faithful.

Prayer:

Dear Holy Father,

We know we are supposed to be secure that You are our provider and know no matter what, we and our families can get through dry periods in our lives, times of need, or adversity. Instead, we fret. We cannot find real faith, though we know You are worthy of it. We cannot find our ability to trust, though we know You, if Anyone, are trustworthy. Please forgive our times of weakness when we insult You with our worrying instead of coming to You for comfort and guidance. We praise You Holy Father for *You* are most worthy of praise.

Amen

8. "You Are My Sunshine"

"You are my sunshine, my only sunshine. You make me happy when skies are gray…."

My mother used to sing this song to me when I was a child. She might be cleaning up the kitchen or folding clothes or completing one of her many domestic duties. It was *our* song we shared together and I cherished it. I later sang the same song to my own children when they were little. In fact, even now, my twenty-three year old daughter and I still love to sing it together with her rich alto voice complementing my first soprano. We don't sound too bad, but that isn't the point.

It doesn't matter how our singing sounds; it is how we feel when we sing this song together that matters. We are celebrating our love.

So where can any of us find sunshine on a cloudy day? There is no use sugar-coating it. Things are rough today, no doubt about it. We turn on the radio and hear doom and gloom. We turn on the television and hear gloom and doom.

We click onto the internet to discover more disparaging news. We wonder if the sun will ever rise again….

Need some Good News?

No matter how dark things get in our lives and in our world, God is in control, and if we will but take a minute to notice, even though we are tense and our nerves are frayed, His Light still shines. The psalmist writes, "For with You is the foundation of life; in Your light we see light (Psalm 36:9).

But how do we find God's light in *today's* world? We start looking first in our own every day experiences. We begin searching for our blessings, noticing the kind things people do for us without being asked, the child who laughs and brings us joy, the loved one who gives us hugs or a comforting word--these are all of God's light, His love extended to us daily.

Psalm 119: 105 declares, "Your word is a lamp to my feet and a light for my path." This is another way we may access God's illumination in our spirits and our lives, through our reading of Holy Scripture. Taking the time to read the Bible ourselves and not just listening to someone else interpret it for us makes all the difference in our relationships with God. It has for me. It's hard for us to have a relationship with God if we, well, for lack of better words, have no relationship. Reading Scripture, I have found, is time well-spent. There's no getting around it if we truly want to be near to God. Asking Him to help us understand what we are reading and what He wants us to take from it *before* we begin our devotional time is a helpful step in the right direction.

Reading the Bible and giving the Holy Spirit a chance to transform us will give us new eyes for reading scripture. He will also enlighten us when relationships or other areas of concern are bothering us and we need His direction. We will begin again to feel hope and faith stir inside us. Further still, we'll be able to shine our love and comfort to those struggling still in darkness who are desperate for the source of the Light we are emitting. Spending time with God is always a wise investment. He is certainly worth knowing better. He is the creator of light in the first place. Talking about sunshine, who is more of a sunshine than He.

Prayer:

Dear Holy Father,

Thank You for being our Light when we feel overshadowed with the darkness of stress, emptiness, and bad news, news that moves from depressing to disparaging. Thank You for remaining firm in Your never-changing Spirit, that we can count on You when there seems there is nothing or no one else we can count on. We praise You Holy Father, for You are indeed always worthy of praise.

Amen

9. "I've Got the Power"

Aren't we all power hungry one way or the other? The one who has the power makes the rules, and the one who makes the rules…rules. Right?

Well, I don't know about you, but sometimes my power is gone. I mess up, it seems, over and over again, and I wonder why I can't seem to get it together. Maybe it is because I'm not meant to.

Not meant to? What kind of cop-out line is that?

When I have felt the most power in my life is when I have admitted no matter how hard I try, my trying is not leading me anywhere but to endless frustration. Finally, I remember God has been there all the time just waiting to be of assistance. But, He is polite. I need to ask.

That's when God's grace kicks in, that is, if I ask for God's help to get me back on track.

The Lord says in His Word, "My grace is sufficient for you,

for My power is made perfect in weakness" (2 Corinthians 12:9). You might wonder, isn't God talking to Paul here in this scripture? Yeah, He is, but His message transcends to the rest of us. That's the cool thing about the Bible. The messages conveyed are for everyone, not just the people in the story line.

When we admit we need God, God provides the grace and power we need to overcome, or certainly deal with in some fashion, whatever the challenges are that have us spinning out of orbit.

It is our choice, after all, in how we deal with our adversities in life. There's a saying that the definition of insanity is doing the same thing over and over again and expecting new results. I think I've had enough of that crazy cycle. Haven't you?

I'm ready for a little sanity in my life.

I'm ready for a whole lot of God in my life.

So, what's our choice going to be? Why not choose grace?

Is there even another viable option out there? Not for me.

No, not a sane one, anyway.

Prayer:

Oh Holy Father,

So many times we do find ourselves in the crazy cycle of making the same mistakes over and over again. We would think we would learn, but we don't seem to. How often we act like we are God and don't need anyone's help--even Yours. If that is not insanity, then what is? Surely it is a whole lot of other things, too, like stubbornness and vanity as well. Thank You for Your endless patience. Help us to hear Your voice and to be calmed by Your loving Presence even when we have no presence of mind to have enough sense to call on Your Most Holy Name. Praise be to You, Father, in the Highest.

Amen

10. "All by Ourselves"

Sometimes, even though I may be surrounded by other people, for various reasons I feel very alone, isolated by my feelings, isolated due to circumstances, and isolated because I tend to be a little "different" sometimes, a little bit too enthusiastic, a little too artsy for some folks….Without a doubt, there are a variety of things that make us feel we are doing it all alone, but we never are, if we will just refocus our perceptions.

The feeling of loneliness chews at our insides, gnaws at our spirits, and leaves us feeling empty and blue. No matter how hard we work to cultivate *real* relationships-not those that are only on the surface and superficial ones- but real ones- sometimes our relationships just do not work out, even with our best efforts. Often when we reach out to others we discover that most people are just too busy, *too busy* to be true friends because they cannot give what they do not have to offer; they are already over-extended as it is and just have no more of themselves to give away. Stinks, doesn't it? We have all probably experienced this type of situation before, or may even be in that same isolated spot right now.

So, if that's the case, where do we find a cure for our blues, a friend for a friend in need? Well, God knows we need companionship. Isn't that why he created Eve for Adam, so he would not feel alone? Just the same, God does not want us to feel abandoned, either. In John 14: 18, Jesus says to His disciples as He attempts to comfort them before His crucifixion," I will not leave you as orphans." Now He is not just referring to His followers there in that room. The message of Jesus transcends to all of His followers of all time. That signifies He means us, too. What that also means is that if we ask God to surround us with His love and comfort us, He will.

Even though I am no longer a child, there is nothing so welcome and all encompassing as the love that is radiated to me from my parents when they each pull me into their embrace. Such unconditional love sure feels wonderful and reassuring.

However, God provides an even greater feeling of warmth and comfort for us all through the genuine love of the Holy Spirit. Jesus promises, "If you love Me, you will obey what I command. And, I will ask the Father, and He will give you another Counselor to be with you forever" (John 14: 15-16). In this scripture, the word Jesus uses for the Holy Spirit in Greek is Parakletos, which means Comforter. Some even say it means Counselor or Helper. Never the less, whether the Holy Spirit is a Comforter, Counselor or Helper, what we do know for sure is that God means for us as His children to feel His presence in our lives. He wants us to understand that He has not abandoned us, no matter how tough or ugly things get. He is there for us at all times.

That's a comforting thought. When our souls cry out in loneliness and despair, feeling abandoned and roughened by the world, God is available to be our Friend 24-7. What an awesome promise God has given us. What a relief that He is a Man who keeps His promises. Finally, Someone we can trust to *never* let us down!

Prayer:

Dear Heavenly Father,

Thank You Lord that we can trust You to be our Companion at all times. Thank You that You never change, so we know You are always that Someone we can trust. We are indeed so thankful for Your unconditional love, and that we do not have to worry about earning Your devotion. There is no way to earn Your love anyway. You have already given it in totality to us.

We praise You Holy Father for Your presence and surrounding love.

Amen

11. “Anything You Can Do, I Can Do Better”

Boy, is the employment world out there competitive. That, of course, is an understatement. Nowadays to stay employed we not only have to be on top of our game, we have to be on top of everyone else’s game, too. That is way too much pressure and way over the top!

“Fine and good,” you might say. “We all like to vent, but, that doesn’t change the way things are. Get in the whining line. See if anybody cares…Nope. I thought not.”

Never the less, being successful at what we do in our work career is important. Bills have to be paid. The Bill Fairy does not drop by our house to cover our incoming bills, and I bet that same fairy does not make an appearance at your house either, right? So, how is a Christian supposed to deal with the highly competitive world in which we find ourselves estranged?

By being humble. Proverbs 15:33 warns, "Humility must come before honor." What that means is, we'd better be careful about tooting our own horns. Being proud of our own accomplishments is one thing. Being *prideful* concerning our accomplishments is something else all entirely.

We all want honors and accolades in the business world. Who doesn't? But, it is *how* we earn those accolades that makes all the difference to God. When we go around spreading gossip, even if what we have heard is the truth, this information is inevitably going to hurt someone at the work place. Is this right? Are we attempting to hide our hopes of knocking someone else down who's rising toward the same ladder we are attempting to climb by wearing the false mask of "concern" as we share disastrous news about others? ("It's because we care," we protest… Sure.)

God does not honor that type of vindictive and

manipulative behavior. If we are doing a good job at work, whatever that means for us (we may be people who work at home for that matter), our accolades will find *us*. We do not need to chase after them or knock anyone out of our way. God has a way of taking care of His own. He will take care of honoring us in His timing to meet His purposes when and if he feels it is fitting. Sometimes it is not the best thing for us to receive promotions or honors. God knows how well we will handle the praise or a promotion. He may just choose to bless us another way instead of the way we are wishing because that is what's best for us. It's all good. God is Good after all.

Prayer:

Dear Holy Father,

Thank You that You do not treat us as we deserve. Thank You for convicting us when we are petty, judgmental or cold in our insensitivity toward others. Forgive us when we casually spread gossip or tell tales at the expense of others. Thank You for Your mercy and Your grace, and help us to be merciful and compassionate toward others, just in the same way we wish to be treated.

In Jesus' name,

Amen

12. "Nobody Knows the Trouble I've Seen"

I was talking to a faith-filled young person last night who has an unashamedly forward approach to sharing her love for the Lord. She cannot help herself. You know how it is with people in love… they cannot resist the opportunity to share their passion for that special someone with others…. Their beloved is their favorite topic and everything that is said in conversation turns somehow again to the love song of their hearts.

This young lady, (let's just give her the alias "Anna,") radiates the love she has for God with a formidable force. No one doubts her sincerity or rebukes her because she hasn't seen many candles on her birthday cake just yet. So how has she formed this powerful bond with God at such a young age? Troubles, my friend.

Last night she confessed, "It is my hard times that drove me into the arms of God. I am so thankful for those times. I have friends who have not been through the trials I have and as a result, they do not have the bond I have with the Lord. I am so thankful that God gave me the opportunity to become so close to Him."

Thankful for the opportunity to suffer? Gee, I don't think I've heard it phrased exactly that way before. But then, again, maybe I have, but I was just not paying close attention. You know that spiritual song that shares,

> Nobody knows the Trouble I've seen.
>
> Nobody knows my sorrow.
>
> Nobody knows the Trouble I've seen
>
> Glory, Hallelujah.

There it is at the end of the first stanza of the lyrics: "Glory Hallelujah." The creator of the song is thanking God for the troubles, the suffering. But now really, why should anyone be thanking God for the very thing we all try to run away from as quickly as possible?

Well, looking back at particular biblical figures can clue us in. How did Paul (Saul of Tarsus) understand that Jesus was the true Messiah? The Damascus Experience right, when he was temporarily struck blind? Or, how did David become a strong and faithful servant of God who was willing to fight the tower, Goliath? Prior to the event he had to stay alone out in nature protecting sheep from bears and lions, and in addition, it appears, he was not treated too well by his older brothers, either. He was persecuted. It was these adversities that prepared him for being a king in the future.

Do we know of others who suffered in the Bible? Do we really have time to discuss all the trials of Adam, Eve, Noah, Moses, Abraham, Isaac and Joseph, not to mention so many others? Surely they were the first members of the official "Sufferer's Club." Did they go around talking about how wonderful it was that they were given the opportunity to suffer? It may sound a little far-fetched, but I think they did in their own ways.

Even in Genesis 3 when Adam and Eve were banished from Eden, God did not abandon them. He was yet with them even though they had rejected Him through their acts of disobedience. Truly, sometimes because of our humanity, our hardships make it easier for us to feel His presence, His comfort. Does this make us shout, "Hooray!" when pain strikes us numb with disbelief and a feeling that we have found ourselves in a surreal, inescapable nightmare? No. I haven't heard any cheers yet from people I know who are reeling right now from trials and slamming adversity.

But, that doesn't mean they will not find their way later to the pathway of discovery that indeed He was holding them all the while, loving them with the fierceness with which only He can love.

Next time pain has me down, I wish I could remember to change the lyrics of the old spiritual if it comes to mind. Maybe I will have the grace to sing the ending, "Nobody knows the trouble I've seen. *Nobody knows but Jesus.*" When my senses scream their sorrow, if only I can just recall that God is supporting me and loving me through and past the darkness and the agony, I will be able to endure it. If I can but remember that God is fully aware of my pain and that He is fully there for me at all times, I know things will go better for me and for those I love. Glory, Hallelujah.

Prayer:

Dear Holy Father,

We will be the first to admit that we run away from pain as quickly as possible. You of All know that we are not the types to yell, "Yes, bring it on!" We actually have to wonder about people who do that…Thank You for not giving any of us more than we can bear, though sometimes, God, at times we think Your expectations are just a little too high concerning our pain thresholds. But, then again, You always seem to get us through it, and we wonder how You have done it, how You have gotten someone weak like us through the madness without going mad ourselves. Thank You for helping us and comforting us, for no one else could ever take Your place as a support. We praiseYour most worthy name!

Amen

13. "Idle Words"

Have we made an idol of idle words? Social networking gives us the chance to chat away effortlessly without much thought. I think that is what gets us, the not-thinking part. And it's not just with the internet either, our mouths get plenty of action as well.

How many times have I said something and regretted it immediately? Or worse, how often have I uttered things thoughtlessly without worrying about the fact that I was complaining, dissing someone, gossiping or one of those other negative "ing" words?

"Nobody's perfect," we might remark and gloss over our digressions without giving them much credit for the damage those actions of chattering mindlessly produce. Yet, Jesus warns in Matthew 12: 36: "But I tell you that men will have to give account on the day of judgment for every careless word they have spoken. For by your words you will be acquitted, and by your words you will be condemned." Jesus took the words we use seriously, and so should we.

Whoever made up that silly statement, "Sticks and stones may break my bones, but words will never hurt me" must have been delusional. Who hasn't had their hearts pierced by the cruelness of someone's word arsenal? I bet no one reading this has gone unscathed. Words can be bullets aimed at someone's self-esteem, reputation, or the essence of the person as a whole.

Jesus also reminds us in Matthew 12: 34, "For out of the overflow of the heart the mouth speaks." Normally we would think that this would be a good thing, to speak from the heart…but not if the heart is filled with vinegar. Jesus uses this reminder when he speaks to the Pharisees, ones who thought they were above approach. Who were the Pharisees? Unfortunately, just like us, more than we might wish to acknowledge. The Pharisees were actually those who were in many cases trying to follow the letter of the Holy laws. They had high standards for others, but for themselves, well, the standards were not always, well, the standard.

We all are Pharisees from time to time. We think we've got the outside of ourselves pretty well packaged, prepared for display to other Christians and maybe even those who are not. We check off the list of religious literature we have been consuming, not to mention popular non-secular tunes. But when the day is done, our accounts fall short.

Everything counts, everything we say or think for that matter. God hears. God knows.

Obviously, If we are going to be held accountable to the Lord for every careless word we utter, we had better get ourselves straightened out. Time is of the essence. Our time to clean out the clutter of our minds and get the trash out of our mouths is now.

Word Up.

Prayer:

Dear Holy Father,

How often do we let words fly out of our mouths without even considering how they impact others? Please forgive us for the mean-spirited, tactless or petty things we have said, not to mention the positive and edifying things we should have said but did not.

Please, Holy Spirit, help us to be a better steward of Your words.

In Jesus' name,

Amen

14. "God Hears Our Fears, Sees Our Tears"

I was speaking to a friend of mine today. She is retired, a widow, and lives by herself. We were speaking in her kitchen while she wrapped up precious lemon bread for me to take home to my family, a treasure indeed, for this treat is moist, sweet, but not too sweet… scrumptious, to be exact. She looked up at me and suddenly shared for no apparent reason, "I was twelve when I was baptized, but I was nineteen before I received the Holy Spirit. Since then I have never been afraid, even though life has presented me with much to be afraid of." I paused and thought about her statement. How could anyone not *ever* be afraid? Fear is something I have not yet conquered, no, not by a long shot.

I agreed with her that having the Holy Spirit as our Companion does make all the difference. I had to admit to myself that I could do better when adversity strikes to remember the fact that I am never alone. God has not left me to deal with trials all by myself. Why do I forget that sometimes when hard times hit? He has not abandoned you, either. In Psalm 102 the author pleads,

> Hear my prayer, O Lord;
>
> let my cry for help come to You.
>
> Do not hide Your face from me when I am in distress.
>
> Turn Your ear to me;
>
> when I call, answer me quickly" (1-2).

Isn't that what we all want, to know that God is listening and that He *will* answer our cries for help and mercy when we are afraid and do not know what to do or where to turn? It is interesting how God works. When I am under duress, and I have prayed for God's answer, so often I hear the answer, the solution for my concern, but it is through the voice of others, people unaware that God is using them to speak to me.

It is obvious that they do not know they are being used as God's mouthpiece at the moment, supplying the words I have been longing to hear. Indeed, there is an intensity about them that stirs my spirit and lets me know from Whom these words of direction are coming.

God is giving me hope, or he is giving me the message to wait and be patient, or He is allowing me to know that He is aware of what is happening and it has not gone past His notice. So, I can find solace that He knows and He will do what needs to be done in His timing and in the manner that He sees fit.

Maybe that's where my anxiety kicks in. What if I don't like what God intends to do? What if it makes me or my loved ones suffer? What if I have to keep enduring painful situations for longer than I can endure?

WHAT IF?

That's when that faith thing/trust thing comes into play. If I knew how everything was going to turn out in advance, it would require no faith, no trust in God to work things out. That's the crux of it all, isn't it? We have to have faith. Either we have faith in Him and surrender our lives to His control, or we don't have faith and try to direct our own lives instead.

Well, I can think of the many, many mistakes I have made when I have tried to handle situations my own way and the disastrous things that have happened as a result, and I figure, maybe I should leave my life and my trials up to God. If He could create the world just with His words as it is presented in Genesis, perhaps God is quite capable of handling the turbulence of my life…yes, even mine.

Prayer:

Dear Heavenly Father,

Thank You for being Someone we can trust, Someone we can believe is faithful to us on all accounts, and always will be. Please help us to surrender our lives unto You instead of demanding that we must have the reins, since we think we know best so much of the time. Forgive us for our ignorance and our arrogance. Thank You for your constant mercy, forgiveness, and grace.

Amen

15. "I'm Waiting, Waiting, Waiting"

Since ancient times no one has heard

no ear has perceived,

no eye has seen any God besides

You,

Who acts on behalf of those who

wait for Him.

(Isaiah 64:4)

Waiting is torture. Anybody in disagreement here? Yeah, waiting is the pits. It hurts when our hearts are broken and we are waiting for healing. It hurts when our bodies are ill or dying and we don't know how to become well again. There's a burning question that haunts each of us: Will God intervene and make me better, or is He going to go another direction? If I think of dying or being chronically ill, am I showing lack of faith?" Those awful, tugging questions all swirl around as we wait, wait, wait, hoping against hope that God will answer our prayers as we desire. We wonder if He will do what we request, maybe, if we show we are willing to wait, wait, wait, earnestly believing that His answer will come, and it will be to our liking.

It says in the above scripture that God will act on our behalf as we wait for His decision, His action or non-action. It's a tough cookie to chew, and even a tougher one to swallow. After all the waiting, we may discover that God has chosen a different route than we ever would have chosen. So then, what?

We trust that God has a reason. God has a reason for how He answers or non-answers as we might see it. God is Good. He is not capable of making mistakes, even if we may want to point out to Him what we feel is an obvious, grievous oversight.

We do not have the mind of God, nor are we expected to understand His thoughts. We are to wait until a time, *if* He sees fit, to allow us an epiphany of sudden insight. Until then, we wait, but as we wait, we trust.

Prayer:

Dear Holy Father,

There is so much pain in the world, so much suffering, and often we wonder, why? Please help us to be faithful in trusting You, especially when we are agonizing over painful situations, and it appears our hopes will not come to pass. Please be our Strength when we have none at all.

We love You Holy Father, and we know You love us, too, no matter what happens.

Amen

16. "How Evil is Evil?"

Everything is relative…that is until we come upon the discussion of the topic of "evil." To what degree of wickedness must we reveal until we are considered evil? That's a tricky one, isn't it?

Paul wrote in Romans 12:2, "Do not be overcome by evil, but overcome evil with good." So there's our directive in how to react to evil, but how do we come to recognize what is truly evil?

Ephesians 6:12 might help us out a little. It explains, "For our struggle is not against flesh and blood, but against the rulers, against the powers, against the world forces of the darkness, against the spiritual forces of wickedness in the heavenly places…." Paul is making it pretty clear. Satan, who is the epitome of sin, is our enemy…not people. Yet, perhaps we do become "evil" when we no longer hear (or wish to hear) God's voice. We listen to our carnal wishes instead and become our own god in our own corrupted minds. If God is

Good and we reject Him, we have rejected Goodness as well; therefore, as a result, how could we become anything but evil without God's goodness? Guess there's no big surprise there.

And true, even though there is a lot of what we would have to deem as "evil" in the world, we must be mindful of Who is in charge. John defines in 1 John 4: 2-3 who we must consider evil, and then he states:

> This is how you can recognize the Spirit of God:
>
> Every Spirit that recognizes that Jesus Christ has come in the flesh is from God, but every spirit that do not acknowledge Jesus is not from God. This is the spirit of the antichrist, which you have heard is coming and even now is already in the world.

That rather spells it out for us, doesn't it? I don't see any room for confusion concerning this scripture. However, John doesn't just leave us dangling there worrying about what the spirit of the antichrist is going to do to us and those we love because he is a strong power in our world. John comforts, "You, dear children, are from God and have overcome them because the One who is in you is greater than the one who is in the world" (1 John 4: 4). That's a nice wrap up. We can relax. No worries! Satan may be powerful, but He is no match for our Father. We know how Revelation ends, right? Enough said.

Prayer:

Dear Heavenly Father,

Sometimes we are surprised by people's lack of conscience, surprised that some people seem so cool with being bad, like being bad is what is right and being good is an out-dated fashion statement. Indeed, there are times when we know we are experiencing an all out frontal attack from satanic forces, and we are shocked at the amount of aggression coming against us and those we love. Father, please help us not to forget that You, for whatever reason, allow these things to come against us for a purpose that is greater and higher than we will ever possibly comprehend. You know why You allow such oppositional attacks. We know we must relinquish our lives to You and trust You in all things. Help us not to be so easily disturbed and to remember that praise for You is always at our disposal, a great weapon against any negative circumstances in our lives.

Amen

17. Where Do I Find Confidence?

I grew up in *The Sound of Music* generation. Kids I hung around with could sing all the lyrics. We could make allusions to the movie during conversations and we all understood the references. Times have changed. But anyway, I remember Julie Andrews' belting out a song from this musical as Maria which was concerning her finding her confidence amidst trying circumstances, and facing her fear of the unknown. One of the lines that boldly states the obvious theme ends with "I have confidence in me!" At this point the character Maria is actually doing a little, "self-talk," trying to have her own little pep rally before she has to meet the captain and his adorable (or not so adorable at the onset) children.

But as much as the director meant well in having the character go through these seemingly positive motions, it just shows that maybe he or the songwriter did not completely understand Christianity, I mean, the character was a nun after all. A nun would have known that we do not find our confidence in ourselves or our own abilities… we find them in God who is the source of our confidence, trusting in His supplying it to us. In reality, Maria, the real nun of whom the movie portrays, would have probably been singing one of her favorite hymns of God's equipping His servants in just this way.

Jeremiah 17: 7-8 states, "But blessed is the man who trusts in the Lord, whose confidence is in Him." That rather covers it. Maybe we could change the song lyrics. Instead of the character's singing, "They'll have to agree I have confidence in me," she could say, "Though they think I am odd, I have confidence in God!"

I think it has a ring to it.

Prayer:

Dear Father,

So often we get everything all messed up. We try to project ourselves and our own supposed abilities into challenging situations without even bothering to consider Your being in the mix. It's like we have You as a back-up plan instead of The Plan from the get-go. Forgive us for our dullness and for once again attempting to put ourselves in Your place. You are in charge and we are not. Thank You for Your endless patience with us. Help us, too Lord, to remember to be patient with others as well.

Amen

18. "Befriend Our Enemies? Really?"

"Bless those who persecute you; bless and do not curse…Do not repay anyone evil for evil" (Romans 12:14-17).

That is something, that scripture above. How are we supposed to fulfill it? I don't know about you, but I have no supernatural powers of my own, so I figure failure is already my destiny if I am expected to accomplish it going solo. Yet, we all, including folks like me, have a Power Source, the Holy Spirit, who will help us out concerning what seems at first glance to be almost absurd expectations here in Romans 12. Thankfully, all things are possible with God.

Certainly, it would be absurd if we had to try and fully forgive people on our own. Thank goodness we as Christians never do have to go it solo. Whew! Even so, sometimes I find myself rehashing what amounts to, if I am honest with myself, petty trifles, things I should have gotten over immediately, instead of rehearsing the offenses in my mind over and over again so the negative thoughts are like a bad movie that just won't go away. Perhaps, sometimes you find yourself in the same situation.

Admittedly, if we have problems at times forgiving others to what amounts to little offenses, how do we get over the big ones and treat our enemies kindly, especially if we think they do not deserve to be forgiven?

Well, there is a bit of scripture that puts us all soundly in our places. Romans 12 has some advice for people who tend to obsess on the errors of others. Paul declares, "Do not think of yourself more highly than you ought" (3). Then he goes on continuing in the same vein, "Do not be conceited" (Romans 12:16).

That obviously seals the case soundly shut for rationalizing un-forgiveness. Nope, no-can-do. No one *deserves* forgiveness. Indeed, everybody sins, even righteous people who try to do the correct thing, and even people who think they have "arrived" to the point they believe they have mastered the Christian lifestyle. Secretly, even though we might often profess humility, we may privately still believe we are a wee bit more superior to those other people who *certainly* need to get *their* acts together….and of course, we know we could hurl them directly to their spiritual mountain tops if they would *only* take our personal suggestions seriously. Oh-oh. So much for deceiving others with our pretense of piety….

So where does this all end? I guess it leaves us at the foot of Christ. He deemed us all worthy of His separation from God and bearing all of our sins even though He had never sinned, not ever, not to even mention what He went through during His crucifixion. That puts us all squarely in the same place as our enemies. None of us is worthy, not a one.

OK, fine, so now what? What can we do to really forgive those who have hurt us? We lift up our lack of forgiveness to God and pray, "Holy Father, You know what this person did. You know how I feel. I offer You my feelings of un-forgiveness and ask for Your ability to forgive so I can be free, free to love, free to live, trusting that You are a just God and know exactly what to do.

That sounds like the perfect solution. In fact, it is.

Prayer:

Dear Father,

You know how hard it is to forgive people who have offended us, especially those who have no remorse and appear to have no conscience. Please help us. We cannot forgive the pain caused by our offenders, and we frankly do not know if we even wish to try. Please heal our anger and our hurt. Please take it away, for only You know how to help us. Please take away our un-forgiveness and replace it with not only forgiveness but ultimately forgetfulness as well. Please, Father, let the memory of the hurtful transgressions of others soften so we are not plagued with the pain of remembrance. We thank You Father in advance, for we know that without a doubt You will help us; the Holy Spirit will be our Comforter. We praise Your Holy Name,

Amen

19. "God is Our Hiding Place"

If you ever played Hide and Go Seek as a child, you might remember how much fun it could be, that is, if you were playing with the right people and had a good location to insure the game was successful. Unfortunately, however, life does not always present us with a "good hiding place" when we find ourselves in trouble or just need to escape from the pressures or anxieties of the world for a little while.

Most of us tend to look for methods of escape by focusing on food, shopping, traveling, reading, or discovering new forms of entertainment-there is an endless list of methods of escapism that could expand to pages, endless pages as a matter of fact!

But, there is only one real reliable Hiding Place. This Somewhere, our Someone, is where we can go and truly find peace and security: Our Father. He is the best hiding place around. That is a fact, not just a lofty opinion that looks rather righteous in print on paper.

Speaking of this topic brings one of my favorite books of all time to mind. It is called *The Hiding Place* by Corrie Ten Boon. It is her nonfiction account of the struggles and trials she and her family went through as a result of hiding out Jews in their home and being involved in the Dutch Underground during World War II. She saw it as an honor to help her Jewish friends and humbly realized her suffering could not possibly compare with theirs. She was a woman of great strength and character.

The reason why I like this book so much is because the author, who is a heroic protagonist in the story, is just an ordinary woman with ordinary hopes and dreams; yet, she is able to persevere through her tortuous experience of being in concentration camps due to her faith in God and His mighty protection. She teaches how God has a purpose for even the worst circumstances in our lives, events that we cannot start to fathom could ever possibly have some redeeming characteristics.

Psalm 32:6-7, which contains the reference of the title of Miss Ten Boom's book, is filled with comfort and strength for those being buffeted by hard times and tumult. This psalm states,

> Therefore, let everyone who is godly
>
> pray to You
>
> while You may be found;
>
> surely when the mighty waters
>
> rise,
>
> they will not reach him.
>
> You are my hiding place;
>
> You will protect me from trouble
>
> and surround me with songs of
>
> deliverance.

What a comfort I find in these words of scripture. Sometimes things do seem hopelessly bleak as we are forced to endure what appears to be pointless suffering we fear may never end. Thank God He reminds us that all is not lost. We shall find hope yet, if we focus on God and allow Him to be our Strength and Source of comfort instead of our trying to be strong and self-reliant to a fault.

He is our Hiding Place, One whom we never have to seek, One we shall ever find, if we but call out for Him and most times, even if we do not call out at all. God is Faithful. Praise be to God in the Highest!

Prayer:

Thank You, God, that You are not like the world. You are not filled with chaos, animosity or despair. You, instead, are filled with a constant love and compassion for our welfare. Oh, how thankful we are to have Your keeping us safe, surrounded by Your love. In You there is always hope that things will someday get better.

Amen

20. "Carried Away by His Love"

Sometimes, no matter how many devotionals we read or sections from the Bible we put to memory, when hard times hit, we still feel utterly alone and overwhelmed with pain, even if theologically we know better. "God, where are You? I need You!" our hearts cry out in despair and fear. Nevertheless, God hears our distress and He answers. He does.

Lately God has placed in my spirit the need to read Psalm 28. That's the way I hear from God; I get a burden or a strong urge. I am not one who hears His voice literally. No burning bushes for me…but still, He speaks. If I am smart, I obey. Who knows how many blessings I have missed because I pretended I heard my own voice instead of God's, and rationalized my disobedience?

One of the most powerful lines in Psalm 28 transfixes me. It contains an idea that is indeed reassuring. The psalmist begs of God: "Save Your people and bless Your inheritance; be their shepherd and carry them forever" (9). *Carry them forever?*

What a comforting concept! Yet, this is more than lovely sensory or concrete imagery-it is literal. Jesus carries us all of our lives, and I would assume that most of the time, we are not even aware.

Again and again God reminds us through scripture that He is sovereign. He is supreme. Nothing happens without His allowing it. Even all the horrible natural phenomenon like earthquakes, floods and tsunamis….as confounding as it may be for a good God to play the key role in these horrific events, He is because He allows them to occur. Yet, He has a reason, no matter how incomprehensible it may seem to us that there could even possibly be anything good in such tragedies.

God is not going to sit us down and provide explanations for everything negative we see in our world or we experience in our world. Our job is to trust God that He has His reasons for allowing the bad things to come to pass and we must trust Him in this allowance. It really comes down to the most basic of faith foundations. We either believe He is a good and sovereign God, or we believe He is not really in control entirely, and as a result, things can get completely out of His hands despite His good intentions.

I am going for the first option. Really, there is no other option at all, not if God is Who He says He is. I have a gut feeling He is all that…and more, much more Goodness and Compassion than we could ever, ever dream of understanding. This, point, when it comes to God's role in our lives, I do understand.

Prayer:

God, thank You for handling everything, especially when things get so tough we wonder how we even remember to breathe. Thank You that You are the Some One we can trust to hear our cries and always care about our daily concerns. How can we ever thank You enough for Who You are? We praise You Holy Father.

Amen

21. 'I'm Covered."

Psalm 32 made its way again into my conscience tonight as the dark was firming in the sky and my mind began welcoming thoughts of sleep. I read this scripture a good bit. It is one of my favorites, for it reminds me that God is my hiding place. But that was not what God was emphasizing for me tonight. Instead, it was the first stanza, one I normally read quickly, trying to move faster to the "good" part, the hiding place part. Not tonight:

Blessed is he

whose transgressions are forgiven,

whose sins are covered.

Blessed is the man

whose sin the Lord does not count

against him

and in whose spirit is no deceit.

I know the beginning of the stanza is critical…Jesus' dying for our sins is no casual matter. I was just thinking about that today, actually, how Jesus was the live sacrifice to atone for our sins. He has each one of us personally covered if we accept Him and proclaim Him as our Savior.

Yet, there is more there. It is in the very last line and it stings me with conviction when I read it. Does your spirit have deceit, I ask myself? I have to stop and give pause. Boy, it would be so easy to rationalize this one away. But, I am not going to. Sometimes I know I omit truths and duck around full answers if I feel uncomfortable that a confrontation may result. Those half-truths, if I am saying them to manipulate or just to cover my own rear, are deception.

It's not a pretty thing to omit. But it is the truth. I would be encouraging a deceitful spirit if I said differently. Thank God I am covered. And true, it is good to confess, but next comes sincere repenting and stopping the committing of acts and behaviors that do not please or glorify God. The Holy Spirit will help me with that. All I have to do is ask. So I am asking.

Prayer:

Dear Father,

You know how we try to kid ourselves that You are fooled by our behaviors-our partial obedience that is really disobedience, our self-serving acts, and our evading telling the whole truth at times to protect ourselves from conflict. Help us to remember that we will be obedient to You if we love You. Obedience means telling the truth without "spinning" our positions with eloquent words or pointed word choice to soften the poor choices we have made or wish to keep secret. Thank You for helping us to be the persons you want us to be, those whose spirit has no deceit and does not take Your covering of sin for granted.

Amen

22." What is the Purpose of My Life?"

"The purpose of my life is to learn to love God more and to communicate that love and grace to others," declares Shelia Walsh from "Vision" in *A Gentle Spirit*, a devotional book for Christian women.

Yet, what is the purpose of *my* life? That's what I asked myself when I read this quote during my morning quiet time I spend in worship. I have had this particular book for years and yet have never had that particular statement strike me like it did at that moment. Bam. It struck me full force. Wow, I thought. I rather like that mission statement. If the two driving forces of my existence are to continually love God and learn how to share that same focus to others through the sharing of God's love and grace, I wouldn't be so me-focused. What a relief it would be to escape the selfish demands and desires of me, myself, and I.

I have been trying to do better. I have tried to work on being more loving towards others and taking out time for others when I really just wanted to be quiet or do whatever it was I had going on without being disrupted.

I bet you can guess exactly how has everything turned out. Yeah, busted. Once again, I have been trying to be better on my own, hoping that God will see that I am trying to be "good" and not repeat my same old sins, but it has not worked. Why did I even think it would? Why? Because achievers achieve and I rationalize that I should be able to be more gentle and less consumed with myself if I just put my mind (my ego is more like it) to it.

I would have saved myself a lot of frustration and probably sin, too, if I had just prayed first and let God lead me in my path toward righteousness. Duh. I can't even find the path on my own, much less walk on it. By myself I just ring around in circles if I even get that far along. Proverbs seems to have a lot of advice for people like me, and even you, too. Proverbs 2 reads from verses 1-6:

> My son, if you accept my words

And store up my commands within

You,

turning your ear to wisdom

and applying your heart to understanding,

and if you cry out for insight

and cry aloud for understanding,

and if you look for it as for silver

and search for it as for hidden

treasure, then you will understand the fear of

the Lord

and find the knowledge of God.

It seems to me that God is stating that if we treasure our relationship with Him by showing our love for Him through our obedience, and asking for help while trusting that He will indeed help us, then God will take away our blindness and help us to understand and have the knowledge of whatever we need to fulfill our purposes concerning His will. Obviously, we not only have to have an intellectual understanding of God, but also a relationship with Him as well, connecting our hearts to our Father. Please Lord, help me apply this scripture to my life!

Prayer

Holy Father,

Often we just feel like bursting into tears due to our frustrations. We want to do what You want us to do, but so often we end up losing our way and feel lost and impeded at every turn. We turn our lives over to You. We give up. We are tired of playing god in our own lives and the lives of others. Please help us to listen for Your voice when we read Your Word and then trust You enough so that when we know You have told us to do something, we will have the faith to believe You have already equipped us in all that we need to be victorious in the plans You have for us. Thank You for Your endless patience and Your constant guidance.

Amen

23. Ready, Set, Go!

What does it mean to be "set?" Growing up in a rural county one might hear people say they are going to "set down for a spell," meaning, that they are going to sit down for a moment. This wording may be quaint, this "setting down," but according to the Bible, being "set" is very important, and has quite a different denotation or meaning to it. Scripture states, "God sets the lonely in families." Well, that sounds very comforting to read about in Psalms 68:5, but what exactly does that mean, to be "set" in this particular context?

I think unequivocally (without argument or debate) it means God knows what we are going through, and He has a plan all figured out to take care of us, so we do not have to worry. We *don't.*

Now the overachiever in me chafes just a little bit with this idea in that I do tend to worry. I worry if I can feed my family if I or my husband lose our jobs or if one of us becomes seriously ill. Then what? Then, God will take care of it, I remind myself. When are you going to get the concept, and not just get it, I berate myself, but accept it and believe it to be true?

Maybe Satan still whispers in the ears of people, telling them that God is not going to provide for them, so they had better get on the stick and take care of the providing before it's too late. Wasn't Eve fretting over eating, if I am not mistaken, worrying about whether God would provide for her needs when Satan reeled her in with the forbidden fruit? Of course, food has always been a problem for many of us, at least for me, anyway. It figures Satan lured Eve with food. Yet, food is not the point. What we need to keep in mind is that the devil does not want us to think we can trust our Heavenly Father. He wants us to be afraid that somehow God is going to let us down. How sad that we allow our imaginations even for a moment to indulge in such hog wash.

Truth be indeed told, God wants us to truly understand that He is a keeper of His promises. He is moment by moment, second by second, aware of all our trials and sadness. Psalm 68: 19 declares,"Praise be to the Lord, to God our Savior, Who bears our burdens." See, God is not just *aware* of our burdens, He *bears* them with us and for us. That was and is what the cross is all about. Psalm 68:20 reminds us, "Our God is a God Who saves." God doesn't just bend his head down through a giant cloud, shake His head, shrug his Almighty shoulders and lament to Gabriel or whatever angel or saint may be nearby, "Gee, it sure stinks to be them! I hope things work out."

No, the end of this same Psalm declares in line 35, "You are awesome, O God in Your sanctuary; the God of Israel gives power and strength to His people. Praise be to God!" God equips us with some of His strength so we are able to overcome any obstacles that come our way, even something as relational as feeling lonely and neglected in a family, or rejected and cast away from those who should love us and accept us. He knows we need love and not just shelter and a full belly.

No matter what the challenge or the conflict, no matter how

minor or major the issue or concern may be, God is there; God is here. And God, surely, surely, is always right on time.

No matter what any devil tries to whisper our direction to confuse or delude us, that my friends, is always the truth. Thank God!

Prayer:

Dear Heavenly Loving Father,

The world is a crazy upside place. The economy has every one freaking out and people live in fear of losing their jobs if not their sanity. Thank You God that You are absolutely aware of everything and that nothing, no nothing, takes You by surprise. Please give us focus and direction so we are not so worried about ourselves and our own personal concerns that we have no compassion or empathy left for others. Thank You God for Your daily provision and that You have a heavenly home already ready and waiting, with no fear of possible foreclosure. You have bought and paid for our eternal dwelling place with Your most gracious sacrifice.

Thank You for Your Peace and Your Reliability. Thank You for Your never changing Love!

Amen

24. "Ready For Deliverance"

You know, sometimes life is just tough. It's not fun, and we have a lot of crud to put up with; in fact, so much crud that the crud is all we can see. It is at these times that we must absolutely stop what we are doing and get down on our knees and ask for deliverance. No, I am not being a little over dramatic. That is exactly what we need to do when life is hitting us so so hard that we feel we are about to go over the edge…and it can happen to anybody.

Psalm 3 knows these times and gets down to it. It states in lines 3-4:

> But You are a shield around me,
>
> O Lord;
>
> You bestow glory on me and lift
>
> Up my head.
>
> To the Lord I cry aloud,

And He answers me from His holy

Hill.

Here God is telling us that He indeed has protection all around us. At times He allows something to get through that wall of security, but He decides when it happens. Even so, He does not leave us alone to deal with whatever the adversity is. He stays right there with us until the outcome has met His will. The "kicker" line (the best) is when later in lines 7-8 the psalm cries out, "Arise, O Lord! Deliver me, O my God!...From the Lord comes deliverance." So there is the promise we can claim. God says He will not allow more to come our way than we can handle, so when we think we have maxed out, it is completely appropriate to call out to God for help. He wants us to ask. We are His children and He cares…more than we can ever or will ever appreciate. We can call for his help right now.

Prayer:

Dear Heavenly Father,

Thank You for honoring Your promise that You will not put more on us than we can bear. Help us to see when we are part of the problem and yet are blind to how we can be part of the solution as well. Help us to be tender to Your answers so we know that You do answer our prayers according to Your will. Thank You, Father, that we can trust that Your will is perfect and that within You lies our Hope for a better today and a better future.

Amen

25. "Seeing Through Eyes of Faith"

"For our light and momentary troubles are achieving for us an eternal glory that far outweighs them all. So we fix our eyes not on what is seen, but on what is unseen. For what is seen is temporary, but what is unseen is eternal" (2 Corinthians 4:16-18). How do we see through eyes of faith if our vision is blurred with tears, or our eyes are opened wide in terror or fear? It's tough. But once we calm down and pray to God for deliverance, provision, guidance, or all three, God will supply it. We just need to ask Him and then know He will honor our requests.

When the Jews were proceeding to enter Canaan and they sent in some to explore and come back with a report, there were two with a positive response, Joshua and Caleb, and then the rest were terribly negative declaring, "We seemed like grasshoppers in our own eyes, and we looked the same to them" (Numbers 13:33). Yet, Joshua's and Caleb's report was quite different and they had been scoping out the very same area. They insisted instead:

> The land we passed through and explored is exceedingly good. If the Lord is pleased with us, He will lead us into that land, a land flowing with milk and honey, and will give it to us. Only, do not be afraid of the people of the land because we will swallow them up. Their protection is gone, but the Lord is with us. Do not be afraid of them."(Numbers 14:7-9)

Hmmm, that is quite a difference in witnessing, isn't it? So what caused the big gap of disparity of faith? Joshua and Caleb were magnifying the Lord, trusting that He would follow through with what He had promised even if they did not have all of the details of how He planned to accomplish it, and the other group focused on the giants and obstacles. One group was magnifying God, and one group was magnifying the obstacles. The results were disastrous for those who did not believe in His keeping His promises. Joy and reward were the consequences for those who trusted in God.

What are we magnifying in our lives, and to whom are we giving our trust? It could mean more than we could ever imagine.

Prayer:

Dear Heavenly Father,

Please forgive us for all the times we have focused on our problems, not trusting You to handle them and trying to handle them on our own. We know we have caused so many problems for ourselves and others because we have not surrendered our lives and its conflicts to You. Please help us to magnify You and believe in Your power and strength instead of worrying about the power of evil and conflict in our lives. Thank You for Your never-ending compassion and mercy.

Amen.

26. "Jesus, Our Warrior King"

I was reading Psalm 24 today when certain phraseology leaped off the page. It rather took me by surprise because it did not fit the paradigm concerning Jesus, that He is the Prince of Peace or the Good Shepherd, these titles that bring a calm and meek picture to mind of our Savior. But a whole other image came to the fore front of my mind when I read this scripture today, text that reveals the Revelation Christ:

> Lift up your heads, O you gates;
>
> be lifted up, you ancient doors,
>
> that the King of glory may
>
> come in.
>
> Who is this King of glory?
>
> The Lord strong and mighty,
>
> The Lord mighty in battle.
>
> (7-8)

This is not a reference to Jesus' riding humbly into Jerusalem on a donkey so people may cry out "Hosanna to the King!" I believe it is referring to another time, the time when indeed Jesus is brandishing a sword bringing His Kingdom to form a new Israel from where He shall reign for eternity. According to scripture, it will indeed be an all-out war, and of course we Christians are already on the winning team. We have no worries on that point.

Though much of the "end-times" talk has been a focal point of the media and has become a popular subject of discussion often among folks, we must keep our focus on the present times and trust our Lord to handle the last days. Revelation begins with the root "reveal." God will reveal His plan as He sees fit and when He sees fit. Instead of being overly concerned about how or when the end of the world as we know it will occur, it is our job instead to spread the news of our Lord Jesus Christ. We must spread our love for our Savior to those who for whatever reason do not know His love or His offer of salvation. Now that is something worth talking about!

Prayer:

Dear Father,

Sometimes we do get caught up in all the end times talk that is the big theme in movies, books and television shows, not to mention countless conversations we find ourselves joining. Thank You that there is nothing for us to be concerned about and that You have it already accomplished. Thank You, Holy Father, that in addition, You fight our personal battles, battles of which we are not even sometimes aware. Thank You, God, that we can always count on You to be our Champion!

Amen.

27. "Exit, Stage Left"

Are you a "flight" or "fight" type of person? Me? Well, it depends on with whom I am having the conflict, actually. If it is someone I am comfortable with, someone who knows all my flaws and peculiarities and loves me anyway, then, I am prone to be more honest with my feelings. Sometimes my "honesty," however, is just an excuse to "let them have it," truth be told, and if I am sitting here typing away on a devotional, I guess I should be telling the truth, right?

Denial only makes things worse. I know sometimes I thoughtlessly vent and puncture others with my word choices. That's wrong, and it is taking advantage of that comfort zone I feel with these loved ones.

But people I am not comfortable with, those people with whom I feel insecure around, well, those are the types I tend to run away from and keep my feelings to myself. I sense the ice is too thin for me to attempt to traverse it, and pretending nothing has happened to offend me is the best route of escape from a potentially bad situation that could easily expand from bad to worse. You know, sometimes this is a good thing, giving ourselves a chance to reflect. Quick responses are not always the best responses.

Indeed, I often realize it was just as well that I chose to keep my thoughts to myself because the person who hurt me was clueless at the time that they were being tactless or rude (you may insert your own pet-peeve offense here in addition). Thus, I decide I just need to get over it and move on. There's a lesson somewhere there- maybe I need to give people I am close to the same show of discernment and swallow back words that are best left unspoken.

Providentially, God gives us an escape route to get out of relational messes when it is not our words that are the problems, but it is those used by others. Psalm 124 hits on situations just like this. It states in lines 6-8:

Praise be to the Lord,

Who has not let us be torn by their

teeth.

We have escaped like a bird

out of the fowler's snare;

the snare has been broken,

and we have escaped.

Our help is in the name of the Lord,

the Maker of heaven and earth.

Yes, sometimes, quite frankly, people do mean to hurt us. They are aware of their aggressive behavior, and what they do is intentional. They feel they have the right to say whatever it is they wish to say under the guise of being "truthful," when probably they are just in the mood to take a few jabs.

At any rate, God states in this psalm that He is the One we should run to for help concerning any occurrences of this nature. He *will* take care of it if we will but trust Him to do so. That's the zinger, isn't it? Instead of fighting, or taking the matter into our own hands, we must run right into God's arms for His mercy and compassion, believing that no matter what, *we will not be dealing with our conflict alone.* That in itself is such a reassurance, the assurance that He will always be there for us…always.

Prayer:

Dear Father,

Please forgive us for the times we speak harmful words to others, feeling it is our "right" to let others know how we feel, even if our words are singularly unkind and tactless at best. Forgive us for taking Your love and the love of others for granted. Please bring to our minds any undisclosed sin we have relating to how we use our words or in any other areas in our lives where we refuse to acknowledge our shortcomings. Thank You that You are our ever-present support and that You understand us better than we will ever understand ourselves. We praise You, Holy Father!

Amen

28. "Blast the Trumpets"

There is something exciting about a trumpet's blast. An important event is about to happen; we are filled with anticipation as we await for the arrival of a well known "star." Suddenly, just as the person steps out into the presence of an awaiting audience, the trumpet sets the stage with magical exuberance. Dah-tuh-duh!!

Yet, at Easter, churches all over the world rejoice the presence of The Morning Star, One who outshines any human who has ever existed on the popularity charts. The instrument sections in sanctuaries explode with joy as worshipers all over the earth cry out, in unison, "He is risen! He is risen indeed!" Certainly, according to Psalm 98, trumpets will blast again before Jesus' Second Coming and announce His fulfillment of biblical prophecies. Lines 4-8 declares:

> Shout for joy to the Lord, all the
>
> earth,

burst into jubilant song with music…
with trumpets and the blast of the
ram's horn—
shout for joy before the Lord, the
King…
Let them sing before the Lord,
For He comes to judge the earth….

Just as we celebrate the resurrection of Jesus with trumpets and all sorts of music for that matter, one can infer here that trumpets will indeed proclaim the return of Jesus to our world. Without a doubt, there are all sorts of signs that "trumpet" His coming is near according to Revelation. Of course, we as Christians need to be alert to those signs. However, more importantly, we need to be careful not to be "so heavenly minded that we are no earthly good." Honestly, I don't think God wants us spending all of our time wrangling through

Scripture trying to pinpoint the occurrence of the Rapture. Instead, I would surmise that He is more concerned with our showing His love with our actions and being kind, merciful and compassionate toward others. Being prepared for His arrival is understandable. But what better way is there for us to be ready for Jesus' arrival than spreading His gospel? I know this is something I need to do better about applying to my own life and testimony.

Prayer:

Dear Heavenly Father,

There are all types of dramatic theories out there in our world about when Your Son is to return. Sometimes it is so easy to get caught up in all of the intensity that surrounds Your arrival. However, we ask that You help us apply Your scripture to our lives so we are not just "book smart," but actually apply what we learn. Please help us to reach out to others and teach Your Gospel with our lives rather than just with our words. Help us not to be overly concerned about what others think about our beliefs and instead worry more about how we can reach others with Your love. We praise You Holy Lord.

Amen

29. "What Grabs Your Attention?"

The world is a fickle mistress. She dances from one lover to the next, switching partners rapidly, leaving trampled hearts behind her without a moment's thought of remorse or pangs of concern about the damage she has willingly inflicted upon others. No, she feels no guilt at all.

According to scripture, in the end times the hearts of people will become cold. Revelation discusses an era when an evil force grabs first the attention and then the adoration of the inhabitants of our earth. It lures victims with what amounts to cheap parlor tricks in the spiritual world, and people are duped into thinking this force is a god. In fact, these misguided folks become even willing to worship this "beast." In Revelation 13 it states: "The whole world was astonished and followed the beast" (3). But I often wonder if this beast has to represent just an individual. Could it instead be a future government as an entity, one whose philosophies seduce the world with its "heroic" acts of humanity toward mankind, pretending to care with a passion that blinds others to its real intent? Will it offer delicious promises of prominence and prosperity for those who worship it as a reward for their servitude? Will it feed on our greed for stuff, so we will do whatever we have to do in attempts to satiate our lust for material goods and status symbols? Is satiation even possible?

There are indeed, a variety of thoughts on this matter being discussed this very minute in homes, offices and places of worship. Tomes of books have already been published on this subject and who can speculate how many books and articles are on the verge of being published even as I write these very word? Yes, everybody seems to have an opinion, but who knows what the truth is?

God does.

God wants no idols before Him today as well as tomorrow. We don't have to read end time prophecy to get that concept. God has stated it many, many times through His commandments and His scripture that we need to get our eyes off of worldly things and upon heavenly things instead. He also warns us that making gods of ourselves, or anything else or anyone else, leads to pure misery, misery for all included, not to mention that it is sin, sin that entraps and destroys us.

Someone once declared, "I cannot see until I get my eyes off of ME." This advice makes a lot of sense. I know I am my most unhappy self when I focus on myself, my needs, and my desires. On the other hand, I feel much lighter in spirit and much happier overall when I pay attention to what is going on in the lives of others and serve them according to God's leading. I have a feeling God is much more interested in our showing love and compassion to others than he is in our judging others. I have no doubt that sacrificial love is the pathway to happiness now and in the future as well. As it turns out, anyway, such love really ends up not being so sacrificial after all. The benefits to ourselves when we reach out to others are astronomical. That way, everybody wins.

Prayer:

Dear Heavenly Father,

It is so easy to get caught up in the frantic pace of our world, so easy to be trapped in the shallow embraces of its materialism. Forgive us when we lose sight of what is important and waste our lives chasing shadows of empty living and consumerism. Help us to remember that You did not put us on this earth to be served and entertained. You put us here to glorify You with our lives. Please reorient us and reset our inner compasses so our lives have a new sense of direction. Please, may we find joy in discovering You and appreciating our time spent with You as well as with those You have placed in our lives.

Amen

30. "God is Our Stronghold"

You know, most commonly when I hear the term "stronghold," it is used in a negative light. I read about praying for God to remove strongholds, things that have either become habitual areas of sin, or behaviors or thought patterns that are moving in that direction in my life, and I forget all about The Stronghold, the one for sure I do not wish to be rid of ever. That Stronghold is God.

I do not know if you have ever read Psalm 27, but it is just jam-packed with awesome reminders that God is our great protector, and in times of trouble or tribulation, He is The Place to turn. Psalm 27:1 declares:

> The Lord is my light and my salvation---
>
> whom shall I fear?
>
> The Lord is the stronghold of my
>
> Life—

of whom shall I be afraid?

All that reassurance is just in the first stanza. God is our light, salvation, our stronghold, and so completely in control of our lives as our Savior, that there is absolutely no one who can touch Him. That is reassuring.

Now, I know what you may be thinking. What about all the lousy stuff that happens to good people? Does that mean God is allowing Satan to "sift" them (or us for that matter), like God allows Satan to sift Job in "Job?" Scripture relates that God sends down rain and sun on both the good and the bad. The same goes for calamities or trials. However, a person of faith has the opportunity to call out for God and He will be the support Person this suffering child of God needs. This Psalm also states, "Your face, Lord, I will seek…You have been my Helper…I am still confident of this: I will see the goodness of the Lord in the land of the living" (8-13). The passage here is clear. All we have to do is cry out for God's help and one way or the other, sooner or later, if we are confident that He not only hears our prayers but He answers them if they coincide with His will, well, we are good to go.

Wondering why I just said "sooner or later" in the above paragraph? Sometimes we do not perceive God's answer right away or it is simply not the answer we had been expecting. Just as I have mentioned previously in the devotional "I'm Waiting, Waiting, Waiting," sometimes telling us we need to wait is God's answer for the time being. For us, the instant generation that has been spoiled by microwaves and instant everything practically in our lives, this is definitely not something on our "to do" list. In fact, it is most emphatically on our "not to do" list, the waiting bit that is.

Yet, if God says this is best, this waiting on Him, it is. He stresses that we must be brave and trust Him. Once again, we have scripture that encompasses the theme of faith, a theme that is repeated over and over again in the Bible.

It also shares in this psalm, "Though my father and mother forsake me, the Lord will receive me" (10). No matter what,

God has unconditional love for us, no matter how many times we mess up. Read the rest of Psalm 27 if you can right now. It is an awesome piece of scripture and a sigh of relief and support for a world that often delivers neither.

Prayer:

Dear Heavenly Father,

The world is often a chaotic, hostile place. Unpredictable events constantly crash around our ears and we cry out to You for relief, hoping you will make sense out of the senseless. Please help us to truly trust You and to lean on the understanding that You know what is going on, even if we do not. Thank You that You are compassionate concerning our tumultuous anxieties and will never, ever abandon us to chance or circumstance. Thank You Holy Father that we may have confidence in You and Who You are.

Amen

Prayer of Salvation:

Dear Lord Jesus,

I now accept the fact that You died on the cross and lovingly took on my sin so that I might spend eternity with You. Surely, Your love is so great for me, You would have made this sacrifice even if it were only for my benefit. Your love for me knows no bounds. Because of You, I have been redeemed. Thank You for forgiving my sin. Thank You that no matter what I have done, how dark my sin has been in the past, no sin is too great for You to conquer with the cross. Please help me to know how to live as Your disciple and to understand how to live my life unto You. I joyfully and willingly take You as my Lord and Savior.

Amen

17608229R00071

Made in the USA
Charleston, SC
19 February 2013